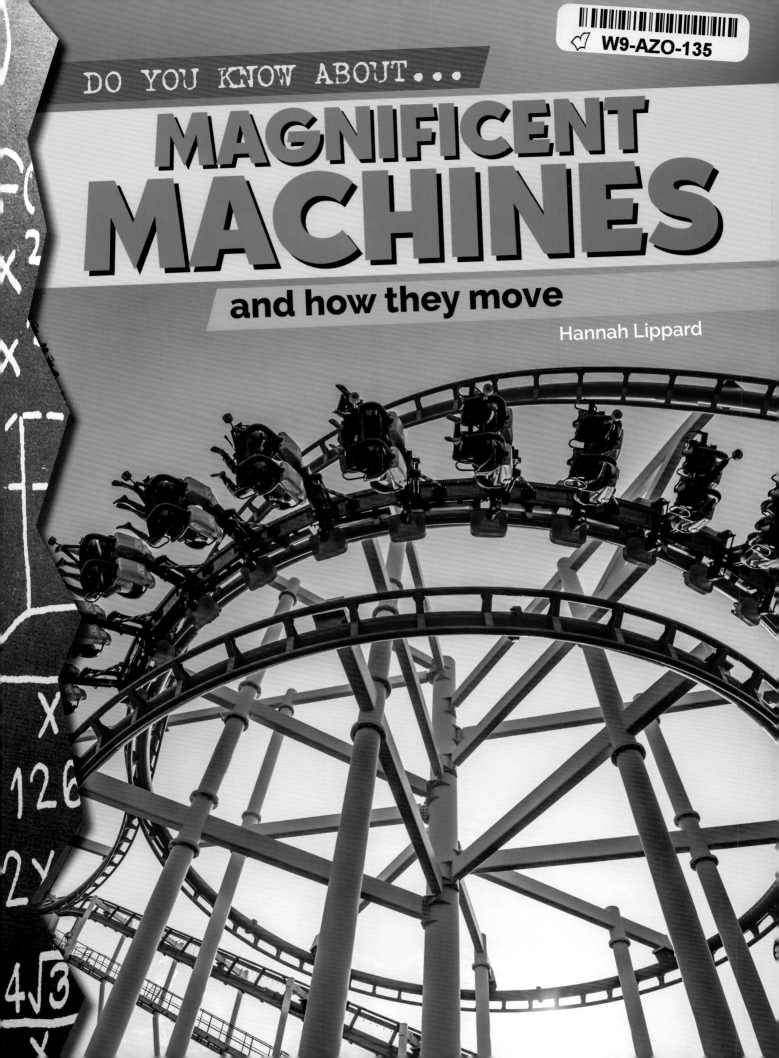

DO YOU KNOW ABOUT . . .

MAGNIFICENT MACHINES

and how they move

Hannah Lippard

Table of Contents

DO YOU KNOW ABOUT....

How much do you know about machines? Find awesome facts throughout the book as you learn more about moving machines that do all kinds of jobs. Just look for Do You Know About... facts throughout the book!

Machines That Move

A machine is a device that uses power to do a task. Just like there are all sorts of jobs—simple and complicated, big and small, serious and fun—there are all sorts of machines to help complete them. Many tasks require movement, so machines need to be able to move, too.

Types of Machines

One common type of moving machine is a vehicle. Some vehicles are used for transportation, like cars and bicycles. Other vehicles are used for scientific research, like submarines and spacecraft. Still others are used in jobs requiring heavy machinery, like farming and construction equipment. These categories also include non-vehicle machines, like robots, telescopes, and machines that plant seeds. Other non-vehicles are used for entertainment, sports, household convenience, manufacturing, and more.

DO YOU KNOW ABOUT...

RGMs

Usually the complexity of a machine is related to the job it does. A simple job requires a simple machine. But Rube Goldberg Machines, or RGMs for short, are intentionally designed to do simple jobs in complicated ways. People build RGMs for fun out of everyday objects to do basic tasks like turning a page in a book or pouring a glass of water. The many moving parts of the machine interact with each other in a domino effect. There are competitions where students can build RGMs to win prizes!

Machine Life Cycles

Machines are not alive like a plant or an animal, but the process of creating and using them follows a path like a life cycle:

1. People have an idea for a new machine to invent. They make a design for the machine and plan how it will work.

2. Prototypes of the machine are built and tested until the machine works like it is supposed to.

3. The machine is manufactured, often in a large factory, and people start to use the machine.

4. More people begin to use the machine, and the machine is improved to make it as effective as possible.

5. The machine becomes less useful as time passes and technology advances, and people stop using it as much.

6. The old machine can be recycled for parts to build a new machine.

DO YOU KNOW ABOUT...

Recycling

Recycling is the process of changing an object that has already been used into materials that can be used again. Recycling machines means that old machines can be turned into new machines instead of being thrown away. It is important because it reduces waste and preserves natural resources. There are three steps in the recycling process. First, the old machine is collected and changed into useful materials. Next, a new machine is built from the recycled materials. Finally, the new machine can be used.

Simple Machines

The six simple machines were defined by scientists hundreds of years ago. They are basic machines with very few parts that can be combined to make many other machines. People used to think that every machine was just a combination of various simple machines. This is no longer true because of modern technology, but simple machines are still important for understanding more complicated ones. You may be able to recognize some of the simple machines in the other machines in this book!

Lever

A lever has two parts: the beam and the fulcrum. The beam is balanced on the fulcrum, so pushing down on one side of the beam sends the other side up. Levers are useful because work requires a combination of force and distance. If you do a job with a short distance, you need more force to compensate. A lever increases the distance, so that a smaller input force produces the same amount of work.

DO YOU KNOW ABOUT...

Moving the Fulcrum

The fulcrum of a lever does not always need to be in the same place. Its position can be adjusted for different types of jobs. For example, to lift an object, the fulcrum should be closer to the object than to the person exerting force on the beam. But to ride a seesaw, the fulcrum should be in the center of the beam so both sides are balanced.

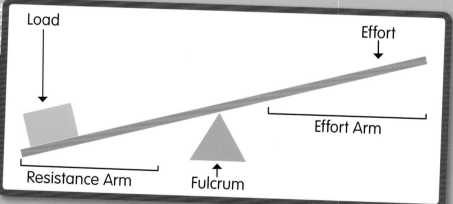

Load · Effort · Effort Arm · Resistance Arm · Fulcrum

Wheel and Axle

Like a lever, a wheel and axle has two parts. Both are cylinders, but the wheel is much wider than the axle. When the wheel is rotated with a smaller force, it results in a larger force on the axle. Wheels and axles can be attached to other objects to reduce the amount of friction between the object and the surface it is moving on.

Pulley

A pulley is a type of wheel often connected to a rope. It is used to change the direction of a force. For example, if you wanted to lift something off the floor by yourself, you would need to use an upward force. But if you used a pulley attached to a rope, you could use a downward force. A system of multiple pulleys is called a block and tackle. Using a block and tackle instead of a single pulley reduces the amount of input force needed and changes its direction.

Tackle Blocks

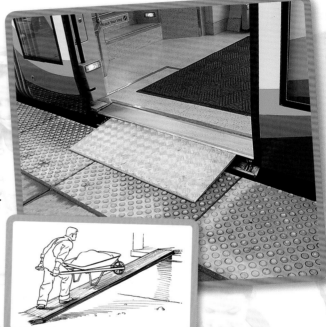

Inclined Plane

An inclined plane has only one component: a flat surface at an angle. Like levers, inclined planes increase distance to allow for a smaller force. Changing the steepness of the inclined plane changes the amount of force needed. A steeper inclined plane requires more force over less distance, and a less steep inclined plane requires less force over more distance. A common example of an inclined plane is a ramp.

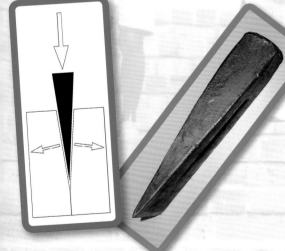

Wedge

A wedge is a small, portable inclined plane. A regular inclined plane is angled on one side and horizontal on the other. On many wedges, both sides are at an angle, making a triangle shape. Wedges are used to lift or separate things. Like pulleys, they change the direction of force. A wedge transfers force against its wide end out both of its narrow sides. The output force is perpendicular to the input force. The longer and narrower a wedge, the greater its mechanical advantage.

Screw

A screw is another variation on an inclined plane. It is a small inclined plane wrapped around a cylinder in a spiral shape. A screw changes a rotational force (the force used to turn it) into a larger linear force (a force going forward in a straight line). Because the spiral inclined plane makes screws grooved, they are easier to insert into something solid.

Screw

Power Sources

Power is the rate that energy is created or used, and energy is the ability to do work. Every machine needs power to work, but different kinds of machines are powered differently. Some machines are even involved in the production of power. They take a naturally occurring energy source and turn it into a different kind of energy. This process is called conversion.

Physical Effort

In physical effort, energy comes from the position or movement of a person. The earliest machines, including all the simple machines, were powered by humans and animals. Many machines still are. These include simple tools like hammers, and human-powered vehicles like bicycles.

DO YOU KNOW ABOUT...

Types of Energy

All energy can be classified as either potential or kinetic energy. Potential energy is energy stored in an object, either because of its position or what it is made of. Kinetic energy is energy that is moving.

Waterwheel

Water

Early water power was in the form of waterwheels, large wheels that rotate when water runs over them. Some waterwheels turn vertically and others turn horizontally. They convert the energy of the moving water into energy that can power another machine. These rotating machines take energy from moving water to generate electric power.

Wind

Windmills have been used for hundreds of years. They convert the energy of air into mechanical energy that can power jobs like grinding grain. Today, wind turbines harness wind power to create electricity. They are more technologically advanced than windmills, with over 8,000 parts. They are usually over 250 feet tall! Wind turns the blades of the turbine, which power an electric generator. Wind turbines are often in groups called wind farms, and the electricity they create can be used to power many other machines.

Wind Turbine

Sunlight

Energy from sunlight is called solar energy. It can be collected using solar panels, which convert the energy into electricity. It can also be collected as heat by a power plant. The heat powers a turbine that creates much more electricity than is available from individual solar panels.

Solar Panels

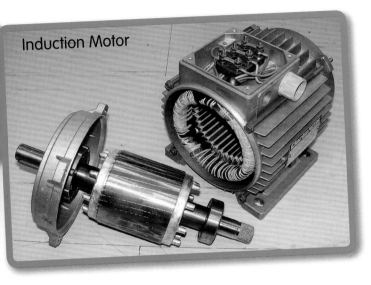
Induction Motor

Engines and Motors

Engines and motors create movement from energy. Therefore, they are found in many moving machines, and there are many different kinds. For example, cars use combustion engines, steam trains use steam engines, airplanes use jet engines, and elevators use electric motors.

Power Plants

A power plant is an entire building (or group of buildings) that creates electric power. It has generators that convert other types of energy into electricity. Power plants usually take up a lot of space. There are many kinds of power plants based on the type of energy they use to create electricity: fossil fuels, nuclear reactions, water, wind, solar radiation, heat from inside the earth, or plant and animal materials.

Nuclear Reactors

Hydraulic Cylinder

Fluid Cylinders

A fluid is a liquid, like water or oil, or a gas, like air. Hydraulic cylinders (using liquid) and pneumatic cylinders (using gas) create motion like engines or motors, but the motion is linear instead of rotational. Electricity is used to send fluid into the cylinder and create movement.

DO YOU KNOW ABOUT...

Renewable Energy

Some energy sources are renewable, which means that when they are used, they can be replaced naturally. Wind and solar energy are both renewable. Other energy sources are non-renewable, which means once used, they are gone forever. Fossil fuels, like coal and oil, are non-renewable. Electricity does not fit in either of these categories. It is a secondary energy source, because it is created by primary sources, like wind or coal, being converted into electric energy.

Space Exploration Machines

Machines are very important for space exploration. Astronauts cannot survive in outer space without them. Many space machines operate without any people at all—their controllers are usually back on Earth.

Rover

A rover is a vehicle that explores the surface of astronomical bodies like planets and moons. So far, rovers have been sent to the Moon and Mars. Because it can take such a long time to send messages between a rover and the people controlling it on Earth, rovers need autonomy. They can navigate by themselves, and in the future, they may have the ability to recognize interesting things in the landscape and investigate them without needing instructions. Rovers run on nuclear or solar power.

Orbiter

An orbiter is a spacecraft that orbits an astronomical body without landing on it. An orbiter can observe the entire surface of a planet as it travels around it. It can also help other spacecraft communicate with people on Earth. For example, it is easier for a rover to send a message to an orbiter which then passes it on to Earth than for the rover to send the message the whole way. Orbiters must be able to withstand being cut off from solar energy when they are blocked from the sun during their orbit.

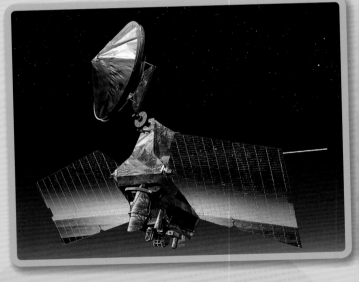

Space Telescope

A space telescope is a telescope that operates from space to study faraway astronomical bodies. The largest space telescope is the Hubble Space Telescope, which was launched in 1990 and is still operating. Its camera has photographed things like clouds and storms over the surfaces of planets and a comet striking Jupiter. Other telescopes operate out of high-flying airplanes over seven miles above Earth's surface. This height helps them avoid interference from most of the water vapor in the atmosphere.

Crewed Spacecraft

A crewed spacecraft is a spacecraft that carries people into space. The astronauts on board are called the crew. The first spacecraft to take a human into space was called Vostok which means "east" in Russian. It orbited Earth once, a trip that took eighty-nine minutes. Two famous American spacecraft were Apollo, which took people to the Moon for the first time, and the Space Shuttle, which was the first spacecraft to be reusable. There are two current crewed spacecraft: Soyuz from Russia and Shenzhou from China.

DO YOU KNOW ABOUT...

Satellites

A satellite is any object in space that orbits another larger object. Orbiters, space stations, and some crewed spacecraft are all satellites. Since they are built by people, they are called artificial satellites. Natural satellites exist too and are more commonly known as moons. They can orbit planets or other astronomical bodies, like asteroids. Many planets have multiple moons. Jupiter has sixty-nine!

Space Station

A space station is an artificial satellite that people can live on and conduct research from. The International Space Station (ISS) is one of only two space stations that are currently operational and is the largest object people have ever sent to space. It was built in pieces from 1998 to 2011. People have visited the ISS from eighteen countries. It is shared by five space agencies from the United States, Russia, Europe, Japan, and Canada. The ISS orbits Earth every ninety minutes. The astronauts working on the ISS conduct scientific experiments and sometimes perform space walks.

DO YOU KNOW ABOUT...

Astronaut Names

Different languages have different words for people who travel in space. The United States, Russia, and China are the only countries with crewed spacecraft, but other countries sometimes send their own astronauts along on American, Russian, or Chinese missions.
• English: astronaut, meaning "star sailor"
• Russian: КОСМОНавТ (cosmonaut), meaning "universe sailor"
• Chinese: yuháng yuán, meaning "universe navigator"
• French: spationaute, meaning "space sailor"
• Indian: vyomanaut, meaning "space sailor"

Land Exploration Machines

Archaeology is the study of people from the past. Archaeologists use machines to search for clues about these people, like human remains, tools, and other artifacts. Volcanology is the study of volcanoes. Volcanologists use machines to explore volcanoes and learn more about how they work.

Ground-Penetrating Radar

Ground-penetrating radar (GPR) devices create maps of the subsurface, the underground area immediately below the surface. Archaeologists use GPR to locate and study areas with buried artifacts or remains without needing to dig underground. GPR works by sending transfers of energy called electromagnetic waves into the ground and then receiving them back. Aspects of the returning wave, like speed, angle, and electrical conductivity, give the archaeologists information about the soil in the area and what might be buried in it.

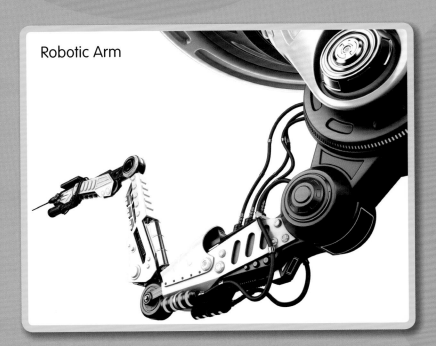

Robotic Arm

Archaeology Robot

Robots are helpful for exploring archaeologically interesting places that are dangerous or inaccessible for humans. For example, some underground burial places in Rome, Italy, are radioactive, so people cannot enter them. Archaeologists can send a robot instead. It is equipped with special sensors to keep it from bumping into things and cameras to photograph what it finds. Robots can also do archaeological tasks that require repetition and sensitivity. For example, a robotic arm can be programmed to make many tiny cuts using tools just like a human arm, except the robot will never lose count or change speed.

Radioactivity

An atom is a tiny particle of an element. The center of an atom is called the nucleus. Radioactivity is caused by unstable nuclei, which means that the nuclei do not have enough energy to hold themselves together. A radioactive element decays gradually and releases dangerous energy called radiation. If humans are exposed to too much radiation, they can become sick or even die, because the radiation kills cells in their body.

Volcanology Robots

Sometimes machines designed for one job can be helpful in another. NASA, the American space agency, plans to use robots to explore volcanoes on the Moon and on Mars. To practice, they built robots to explore volcanoes on Earth. The robots are called VolcanoBots and they can fit into small openings in volcanoes that humans cannot. The robots could help scientists learn more about how volcanoes erupt, like tracking the path taken by magma during an eruption. So far, the VolcanoBots have been tested on Kilauea, a volcano in Hawaii.

Kilauea

Volcanic Activity

Kilauea is an active volcano—a volcano that has erupted in the past 10,000 years—that last erupted in 2018. Volcanoes can also be classified as dormant or extinct. A dormant volcano has not erupted in the past 10,000 years, but people expect it to erupt again. An extinct volcano has not erupted in 10,000 years and is not expected to erupt again.

Water Exploration Machines

Underwater research can be very dangerous for human divers. Using robots to collect information is safer and more efficient. But not all machines used in water research are built for safety. Some are invented in order to better understand aquatic ecosystems.

Autonomous Underwater Vehicle

An autonomous underwater vehicle, or AUV, is an underwater robot similar to a rover. It navigates and powers itself without human direction. Usually AUVs are battery-powered, but some are solar-powered and spend time near the surface of the water to charge. AUVs can work in shallower water than boats and deeper water than people. They have sensors that help scientists map the ocean floor, locate underwater objects or natural formations, and study the marine environment.

Blackghost AUV

AUV URASHIMA

DO YOU KNOW ABOUT...

Types of AUVs

Originally, all AUVs were long and cylinder-shaped. Now there is a large variety of AUVs. Some weigh under 100 pounds and some are thousands of pounds. Some are used in one area, and some can move between the surface and nearly 20,000 feet down into the sea. Some can hover in the air above the water like a helicopter.

Remotely Operated Vehicle

A remotely operated underwater vehicle, or ROV, is an underwater robot with less autonomy than an AUV. It is usually connected by cables to a ship on the surface, where a person controls its movement with a joystick. ROVs have cameras and lights so that they can take pictures and videos underwater. Sometimes they also have technology for collecting samples and taking measurements. They can be as small as a computer or as large as a truck. They are very maneuverable.

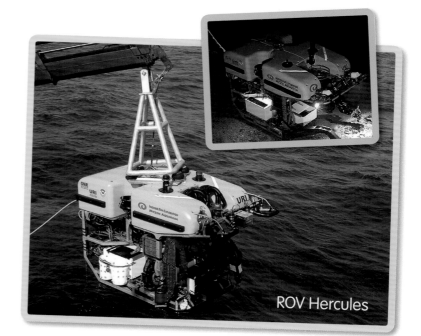

ROV Hercules

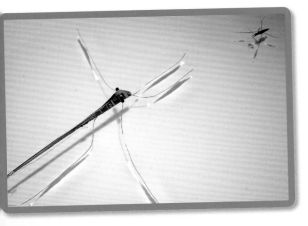

Robostrider

Robostrider is a small robot designed to move like a water strider, an insect that can walk on water. Researchers built the robot while studying how the water strider moves. Formerly, scientists thought water striders made waves that propelled them. Now they know that they move over the surface of water using a rowing motion, as if their legs were oars. Robostrider was engineered to move in the same way.

OceanOne

OceanOne is a humanoid robot that can dive over 300 feet underwater without being damaged from the high pressure like humans would be. People on land control its movements, and it has AI, or artificial intelligence, to help it navigate. OceanOne has special sensors that collect data about its environment, including touch sensors on its hands. It can explore underwater sites, like shipwrecks, or use tools underwater to build and fix things.

DO YOU KNOW ABOUT...

Artificial Intelligence

Artificial intelligence is the ability of a machine to act and think in a similar way to humans. People program machines to have this ability. To be truly "intelligent," a machine would need to be able to learn and adapt the way humans can. Sometimes with advances in AI, researchers understand human intelligence better.

Trains

A train is a type of vehicle that moves on tracks, also called rails. It is made up of two or more individual units connected to each other, called cars. Trains need to be specialized for the type of job they do. They can travel short or long distances, move at fast or slow speeds, and run on the ground, above it, or below it!

Rapid Transit

Rapid transit trains are trains like subways and metros. They are usually found in urban areas. Their tracks are either underground or aboveground to separate them completely from road traffic. Rapid transit trains are named for their speed, which is possible because they are designed to reduce air resistance. They travel at about sixty-five to seventy miles per hour.

DO YOU KNOW ABOUT...

Types of Tracks

Not all train tracks are alike. Common railways can be found around the world and were the first type of track when steam trains were invented. Electrified railways power the train using electric currents in the rails. High-speed rails are specially designed for carrying high-speed trains. Maglev, or magnetic levitation, railways use magnets to lift and move the train. Finally, monorails have only one rail instead of two. They are usually used by slower trains, and sometimes the trains run underneath the tracks!

Maglev Railway

Light Rail

Light rail trains are also called trolleys, trams, and streetcars. They are used for local transportation in cities. They move more slowly than rapid transit at about fifty-five to sixty-five miles per hour. Unlike rapid transit, light rail trains travel on the street at the same level as road traffic, but the trains use a different part of the road. Sometimes light rail trains move slower closer to the center of a city where there is more traffic, and they might stop every few blocks. They are usually powered by electricity from wires that run above them.

Commuter Rail

Commuter rail trains connect cities and suburbs. They are mainly for people who live outside the city but work inside it. Commuter trains work differently in different countries. In the United States, the passenger cars are usually pulled or pushed by a locomotive powered by diesel fuel or electricity. In Europe, multiple cars—or all the cars—usually have their own engine. This makes it easier to change the length of the train. European commuter rail trains tend to weigh less than American ones.

Seattle, Washington

Intercity Rail

Intercity rail trains carry passengers between different cities. They can travel distances as far as airplanes. However, they move much more slowly (about the same speed as road traffic) and they stop at small cities that airplanes would fly over. Intercity rail can run on land or underground. The trains may include special cars for sleeping and dining, because the journey is longer than on other trains.

High-Speed Rail

High-speed rail trains travel at ninety miles per hour or faster. They connect cities like intercity rail, but they do not make as many stops and their travel time is comparable to that of airplanes. High-speed rail trains are used in many European and Asian countries. They run on special tracks that enable them to move faster and more smoothly.

DO YOU KNOW ABOUT...

Underwater Trains

A high-speed train called Eurostar travels between London and Paris underwater. It moves through a rail tunnel called the Channel Tunnel (or Chunnel) which connects England and France via the English Channel.

Automotive Road Vehicles

Automotive road vehicles are self-propelled, which means they carry their power source inside them. They travel on roads, sometimes with other types of vehicles, like light rail or human-powered machines. They all have motors or engines, and they have transmissions to change these devices' speeds.

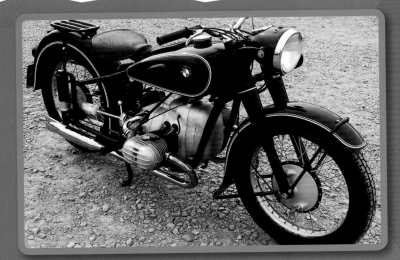

Motorcycle

A motorcycle is a vehicle with two (or sometimes three) wheels, one in front of the other. It is like an automotive version of a bicycle. Motorcycles usually have a frame made out of steel and tires that are smaller and more rounded than car tires. Their shape allows the motorcycle to lean to the side when turning. Motorcycle transmissions have up to six speeds.

DO YOU KNOW ABOUT...

Transmissions

A transmission changes the speed of the engine: a higher speed when the vehicle needs more power and a lower speed when the vehicle needs less. The transmission is located between the engine and the wheels. It works by transferring the engine's rotational force (called torque) to the wheels. A driver can control the transmission using a device called the shift lever.

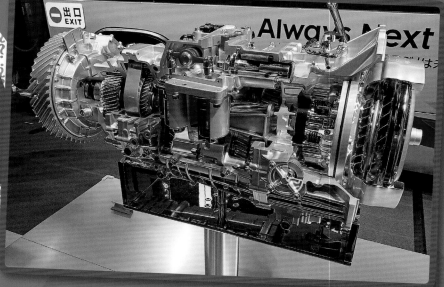

Car

Cars are four-wheeled vehicles. Most cars use internal combustion engines which work by burning gasoline fuel to convert chemical energy into mechanical energy. Cars also need oil to reduce friction between the different car parts and cooling systems to keep them from overheating. Car transmissions can be automatic (changing speeds by themselves) or manual (needing the driver to change the speeds).

Bus

Buses are large vehicles used to carry more than ten people. They have diesel internal combustion engines which are more powerful than gasoline engines. Buses are often part of public transportation. They have more flexible routes than urban trains since they don't need tracks, and they can share the main part of the road with cars. Some buses are articulated, which means they have multiple frames connected to each other, letting them bend when they turn. Others, called double deckers, have two floors. School buses carry students to and from school, and they often have special safety and visibility features, like yellow paint.

DO YOU KNOW ABOUT...

Hybrid and Electric Vehicles

Not all cars use gasoline. Instead they are powered by electric motors and rechargeable batteries. Electric cars are better for the environment, because gasoline is a non-renewable resource and it pollutes the air. There are also hybrid cars, which use a combination of a gasoline engine and an electric motor. Hybrids use gasoline to recharge their batteries and to provide power when electricity is not enough.

Charging Station

Truck

A truck is a vehicle that transports objects (rather than people) or is used for a special purpose, such as a fire truck. Like buses, trucks have diesel engines and can be articulated. The front part of a truck is called the truck tractor. This is where the driver sits and the engine is located. The back part is called the truck trailer. This is where the load is carried. The trailer and tractor are attached, and the tractor pulls the trailer. Truck transmissions can have up to eighteen speeds!

Boats

Boats are watercraft, or vessels, that move on water. Boats are usually smaller than ships. They have a variety of power sources: human effort, wind, or engines.

Canoe

A canoe is a small human-powered boat. It has a narrow and light hull, or frame, and is propelled by paddling. A paddle is a wooden tool with a long round handle and a flat wide blade. Pushing or pulling the blade against the water moves and steers the canoe. Canoes have existed for thousands of years. Today they are built out of a variety of materials: wood, canvas, aluminum, fiberglass, and more. Other human-powered boats include gondolas, which are propelled by rowing with oars, and pedalos, which are propelled by peddling.

Sailboat

Sailboats are propelled by the wind. Their sails catch the force of the wind, and a device called a rudder is used to steer them. Sailors must adjust the sails and move the rudder to adapt to changes in the wind's speed and direction. Sailboats also have boards underneath them called centerboards that keep them from tilting too far to the side. Large sailboats sometimes have engines in addition to sails, in case there is not enough wind to propel them. Sailboats can be seven to seventy feet long. Some sailboats, called catamarans, have two hulls.

Tugboat

A tugboat is a small but strong boat with a diesel engine that is used to pull and push other boats, usually much larger ones. Tugboats can help ships move in narrow waters, like harbors and rivers, in a process called tug assist. They move using propellers, which makes them more maneuverable. Sometimes tugboats also help in firefighting missions.

DO YOU KNOW ABOUT...

Displacement

A boat on the surface of water moves some of the water out of the way, which is called displacement. The displaced water weighs as much as the boat does. Displacement creates buoyancy, a type of force. Buoyancy works in the opposite direction of gravity, pushing the ship up instead of pulling it down.

Lifeboat

There are two types of lifeboats: shipboard lifeboats and rescue lifeboats. Shipboard lifeboats are carried on a ship. They are very small. If there is an emergency, the crew and passengers can use them to escape, and they carry basic supplies like food and water and first aid kits. Rescue lifeboats are larger and not part of a ship. They are used to rescue people in danger at sea, either from another boat or from the water. Lifeboats may be propelled by oars or engines.

Rescue Lifeboat

Ferry

Ferries are passenger boats. They usually travel short fixed paths, carrying people from one side of a body of water to the other. Ferries are especially useful where the water is too dangerous to build a bridge or tunnel to cross it. Most ferries carry cars as well as people, so that when the people arrive on the land at the other side, they have a car ready. Many ferries move slowly, but some are engineered to travel at high speeds. These ferries are narrow and pointed to help them move faster, and they use high-speed diesel engines.

DO YOU KNOW ABOUT...

Submarine Density

Submarines can control their buoyancy to sink or rise in the water using special tanks. Filling the tanks with air makes the submarine less dense than the water around it, so it floats. Filling the tanks with water makes the submarine denser than the water around it, so it sinks. Creating a balance of air and water in the tanks makes the submarine's density the same as the water around it, so it stays at the same depth.

Submarine

Submarines travel entirely underwater, and they may not surface for up to six months. They are usually used by militaries. Since they stay below the surface, they can avoid being seen. Submarines can attack ships or land targets using torpedoes and missiles. Usually they can launch their weapons without rising to the surface.

Ships

A ship is a large vessel that travels in the ocean. One of the main differences between boats and ships is size. Often boats can be carried on ships, but not the other way around. Additionally, ships usually have permanent crews and travel on the open ocean where the water is deep. Boats usually only have crews when they are being used and stay closer to the shore.

Dry-Bulk Ship

Cargo Ship

A cargo ship is a ship that carries cargo, like materials or products, instead of passengers. Cargo ships carrying liquids are called tankers, because they consist of multiple tanks inside a hull. Cargo ships carrying dry products like grain are called dry-bulk ships. They have big hatches for loading and unloading the cargo. There are even cargo ships that transport large shipping containers or other ships.

DO YOU KNOW ABOUT...

Propulsion
Modern ships are usually powered by engines. They have paddle wheels or propellers at the aft (back). A propeller is like a huge fan that spins underwater. When it turns using power from the engine, it pushes water back and the ship moves forward. The propeller's force on the water results in thrust from the water resistance.

Paddle Wheel

Propelle

Icebreaker

Icebreakers are ships used to cut through ice. They are usually wide but sloped toward the bow (front). This makes the ships wedge-shaped, so they can better break into the ice. Icebreakers need a lot of power to be stronger than the ice resistance. They also need special protection for their propellers and hull. The hull has extra layers at the waterline so that the ice does not damage it. Icebreakers are often owned by governments and used in scientific research.

Cruise Ship

Cruise ships developed from ocean liners, which were used for overseas transportation before airplanes. Unlike ocean liners, cruise ships are used primarily for entertainment. They hold thousands of passengers, so they have many decks. They also have modifications to make them more comfortable. They dampen the noise of machinery, reduce the rolling movement of the hull, and usually have white paint to reflect sunlight and keep the decks cool.

 DO YOU KNOW ABOUT...

The *Titanic*

One of the most famous ocean liners was the RMS *Titanic*. It sank in 1912 after hitting an iceberg in the Atlantic ocean. Its hull was larger than any moving object humans had built before. The *Titanic* may have sunk because of an engineering problem that allowed water to move between compartments in the ship. It is also a tragic example of the importance of lifeboats. There were more than 2,240 passengers and crew on the ship, but only enough lifeboats to carry 1,178. Over 1,500 people died.

Aircraft Carrier

An aircraft carrier is a warship, or a ship that is a part of a country's navy. Aircraft carriers are basically moving airbases in the ocean. Airplanes and helicopters can land on and take off from them. The aircraft operate from the flight deck, which is the top deck of the ship where the runways are located. Aircraft carriers are the biggest type of warship. They can weigh over 100,000 tons and carry eighty aircraft at a time.

Destroyer

A destroyer is a small warship that can attack land targets and defend against attacks from planes, ships, and submarines. It carries weapons like missiles, guns, and torpedoes. Destroyers move quickly and are easily maneuvered. They are usually used as support and protection for bigger ships, but they are not limited to battle. They also act as protective escort ships during peaceful water travel.

Aircraft

An aircraft is a machine that flies in the air. Aircraft have similarities with watercraft because both machines move through fluids—aircraft through air and watercraft through water.

Airplane

An airplane is a heavier-than-air aircraft with landing wheels and fixed wings, which means the wings cannot move independently of the plane. The shape and position of the wings causes the air below them to move slower than the air above. Slower air exerts more pressure than faster air, so the air beneath the wing pushes on it more, causing the airplane to fly up. This is called lift. Modern airplanes most often use jet engines, which collect air and use fuel to ignite it. The combustion produces thrust. Some airplanes fly so quickly that they move faster than the speed of sound.

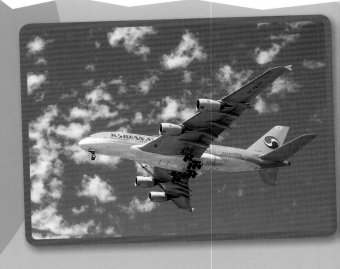

DO YOU KNOW ABOUT...

Aircraft Density

An important difference between types of aircraft is their density in relation to air density. Heavier-than-air aircrafts need an energy source that can create thrust. Lighter-than-air aircrafts rise and float simply because they are lighter than air, but they may have engines to control the direction and speed they move in.

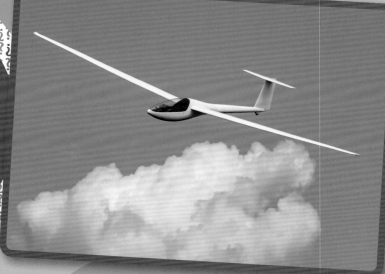

Helicopter

A helicopter is a heavier-than-air aircraft that can fly both horizontally and vertically. It can also hover, or stay in the air without moving in any direction. This is possible because of the propeller attached to the top. Unlike ship propellers, a helicopter propeller is actually a pair of wings that rotate together to create lift. A helicopter usually has a second propeller on its tail that rotates in the opposite direction to keep the machine stable. Helicopters use jet engines like airplanes, but instead of wheels they generally have landing skids, which are tubes that slide against the ground.

Hot-Air Balloon

A hot-air balloon is a lighter-than-air aircraft that, like ships, relies on buoyancy to float. It will not rise unless the air inside the balloon is less dense than the air outside. Hotter air is less dense than cooler air, so heating the air inside the balloon makes it float. To make the balloon go down, the hot air is released through vents on the top. People ride in the basket under the balloon, which the burners are attached to. The balloon itself must be made from fireproof fabric to avoid catching fire from the burners, which heat the air to about 212 degrees Fahrenheit!

Airship

Airships are like balloons that can be steered. Unlike balloons, they have engines, rudders, and propellers. Today people use airships called blimps for advertising. They are not very popular for travel because modern airplanes move so much faster. The largest airship ever was called the Hindenburg and could carry one hundred people. It used hydrogen gas, which exploded and destroyed the airship, killing thirty-seven people. Today, airships use helium gas, which is safer because it does not explode. An airship's material can be rigid (more common in the past) or balloon-like (more common now).

Glider

A glider is a heavier-than-air aircraft similar to an airplane but lacking an engine. It is launched from a high place to start its flight. Gliders can use warm rising air to glide upward, or they can just float forward and down. They do not create thrust like airplanes since they lack engines, but they can still have lift and be slowed down by drag. There are different kinds of gliders. Hang gliders have cloth wings and are very simple machines. Sailplanes have parts similar to airplanes except for the engine.

Hang Glider

Drone

Drones are heavier-than-air aircrafts that do not carry people. They are also called unmanned aerial vehicles. They can be controlled from the air or ground and are usually used by scientists or militaries. Drones function in places where flying machines with humans on board would be dangerous. They can collect information to send back to their controllers, or they can attack with missiles and bombs.

Human-Powered Vehicles

Human-powered vehicles are powered solely with mechanical energy from human muscular effort. They are usually designed to transport a single person. Human-powered vehicles reduce pollution because they never require fossil fuels. They are used for transportation and mobility, entertainment, and sports.

Bicycle

A bicycle has two wheels and a frame of hollow tubes that distribute the weight of the rider throughout the machine. It is propelled with pedals and steered with handlebars. Pedaling a bike turns its wheels, and gears can be used to make the bike travel further for each rotation. A cyclist has to provide force greater than opposing forces like gravity and air resistance. About 90 percent of the energy a rider uses to pedal is converted into kinetic energy. This is more effective than engines and motors, even though bicycles cannot move as fast as vehicles powered with those machines. About 130 million bicycles are built every year!

DO YOU KNOW ABOUT....

Wheel Sizes
Bicycle wheels are usually taller than car wheels, at about twenty inches in diameter for a standard road bike. Racing bikes have larger wheels, because larger wheels tend to make a bicycle go faster. Mountain bikes have smaller wheels, because smaller wheels make it easier to go uphill.

Racing Bike

Mountain Bike

Skateboard

A skateboard has only three parts: the board (called the deck), the wheels, and the devices that connect the wheels to the board (called the trucks). Skateboard wheels are made out of a material called urethane, which keeps them from losing energy. They rotate when a skateboarder kicks against the ground to push forward and then balances on the board. Skateboards can be used to do tricks like turns, jumps, and flips.

Roller Skates

Roller skates are shoes with wheels attached to the bottom. They also have devices called bearings, which help the wheels rotate more smoothly. Bearings make it easier to turn and curve. There are two kinds of skates: traditional roller skates with the wheels in a rectangular arrangement and inline skates with the wheels in a row like a blade. Roller skates work because rolling creates less friction than sliding, and friction slows an object down.

Inline Skates

Ice Skates

An ice skate is similar to a roller skate except it is designed to work on ice instead of land. The shoes have blades positioned like the wheels of an inline skate. The blades glide over the ice with very little friction. Ice skaters propel themselves by pushing forward off of the ice. They lean forward to accelerate. This keeps them balanced and reduces drag.

Wheelchair

Wheelchairs are designed for use by people who cannot walk easily or at all because they are sick, injured, or disabled. A manual wheelchair is moved by turning the wheels with the hands or by a second person pushing it from behind using handles. Some wheelchairs roll on sand and in shallow water, so they can be used on beaches. Other wheelchairs are specially designed for athletes.

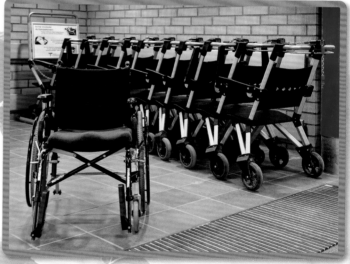

Rail Bike

A rail bike works a lot like a bicycle in that the rider powers the rail bike by using pedals. A major difference between a rail bike and a regular bike is that a rail bike is ridden on a railroad track. Rail bikes can typically hold two to four people and are most often used by tourists to explore a scenic area.

Electric Personal Transporters

Like human-powered vehicles, electric personal transporters are small vehicles generally designed for a single person. Many of them are electric versions of human-powered vehicles. They are powered by a battery and an electric motor, which converts the energy stored in the battery into motion.

Electric Scooter

An electric scooter is similar to a non-powered scooter, except that a battery and electric motor help power it. The rider still kicks against the ground, but less force is required. Electric scooters have sensors to detect the speed of the back wheel. When the wheel's rotation speeds up after a kick, the motor assists in increasing the speed. When the rider brakes, the motor reverses to recharge the battery and slow down the scooter.

DO YOU KNOW ABOUT...
Engines and Motors

The words "engine" and "motor" are often used interchangeably, and both devices provide motion. However, they have slightly different meanings. In general, an engine changes the chemical composition of the fuel it uses as an energy source. A motor does not. Electric personal transporters have electric motors.

Electric Skateboard

An electric skateboard is a skateboard with a battery and motor underneath the board, so that a skateboarder can ride without pushing off against the ground. Electric skateboards can travel six to twelve miles at a time at speeds up to twenty-two miles per hour. The skateboarder controls their direction with a wireless device in their hand. Electric skateboards have small wheels that are only suitable for roads.

Self-Balancing Scooter

Self-balancing scooters are often called hoverboards, but they do not actually hover or fly. They roll on two wheels that hold electric motors and sensors to detect the speed and tilt of the wheel. The more a rider leans forward, the faster the wheels turn. On top of the board are two pads that a rider stands on. The pressure of the rider's feet activate switches that spin the wheels. A Segway is a variation of the self-balancing scooter with handles for stability.

Hoverboard

Batteries

A battery is a collection of devices called electrochemical cells that make chemical reactions to create electricity. Because of their electrochemical cells, batteries are portable storage for potential energy that can be used when needed. This makes them very useful for machines that move.

Self-Balancing Unicycle

Self-balancing unicycles work similarly to self-balancing scooters. They have pads and sensors, and they are controlled by leaning forward to accelerate and backward to decelerate. But self-balancing unicycles have only one wheel. It is large, usually twelve to sixteen inches, so it works on grass, dirt, gravel, and even in puddles. Depending on their batteries, unicycles may be able to travel for as little as four miles or as many as fifty miles at a time.

Construction Equipment

Construction equipment is a type of machine used for building projects. There are different types. Earth-moving equipment, like bulldozers, excavators, and loaders, can move dirt and soil at a construction site. Material-handling equipment, like cranes, can move and lift other objects. Construction equipment, like compactors, are involved in the building process.

Bulldozer

A bulldozer is a crawler: a tractor machine that moves on tracks of chain belts instead of wheels. It has a wide blade attached to its front that is used to move large amounts of dirt. The blade's movement is controlled by cylinders called pistons. Bulldozers are so heavy that they can also be used to crush boulders. They are one of the most powerful construction machines.

Excavator

An excavator is like a huge powered shovel. It consists of a cab which can be on wheels or tracks and a long arm with a bucket at the end. The cab turns all the way around so that the excavator can dig in any direction. The arm uses hydraulic power to move. Excavators usually dig dirt or lift heavy items like pipes. They are useful for both small and large construction projects. They can even drag their arms along the bottom of rivers to lift out sediments.

Crawler Loader

Loader

A loader is a machine used to load materials onto another machine. There are different types of loaders, but they all consist of a bucket for carrying materials, a moving arm, and a cab or tractor. Backhoe loaders have buckets in the back and shovels in front. They move on four wheels. Crawler loaders move on tracks. Skid-steer loaders are smaller than the other types and useful for maneuvering in smaller areas or areas where construction is nearly complete and a bigger machine could cause damage.

Crane

A crane is a tall machine used to move heavy objects. Cranes usually have ropes or chains and special pulleys called sheaves for lifting and lowering. They also have an arm that extends near their top, which is called a jib. In addition to construction, cranes are useful for manufacturing or transportation tasks which require moving heavy objects. Depending on the job these are being used for, cranes can range in size from small jib cranes to large tower cranes.

Tower Crane

DO YOU KNOW ABOUT...

Wheels and Tracks

Some construction machines use wheels, while others use tracks. Wheels are faster and more maneuverable than tracks, but they have to be very large to drive over an obstacle. Tracks create more friction with the ground so they are better at moving over rough terrain and obstacles, but they are less maneuverable and slower than wheels.

Wheel

Tracks

Road Roller

Compactor

A compactor is a machine that presses on a material to make it denser. This is important because it allows a surface to be able to support a structure built on top of it. There are three types of compactors. Road rollers have large rollers that compact roadbeds, the bottom layer of roads. Plate compactors have vibrating plates that make a surface level instead of sloped or uneven. Jumping jack compactors are used to compact materials in smaller spaces, like holes for pipes.

Agricultural Equipment

Agricultural equipment is used to grow crops. There are multiple steps in the farming process: preparing the soil, planting the crops, taking care of them while they grow, and harvesting them when they are ready. Machines can help with these tasks.

Tractor

A tractor is an automotive vehicle that can have either wheels or tracks. Tractors are used to pull or attach to other machines, called implements. They have powerful diesel engines, like trucks and buses, but they do not use their engines to go fast. Instead they use them for pulling heavy machines behind them or for providing power to the machines they attach to.

DO YOU KNOW ABOUT...

Tractor Implements

Implements are attached to a tractor using a strong rod on the tractor called a drawbar. They can be raised and lowered using a device called a hydraulic hitch. This makes it possible to lower the implement during work and then raise it to transport it somewhere else. Implements are powered using the power takeoff, a rod that rotates about 500 times per minute and transmits power from the tractor's engine.

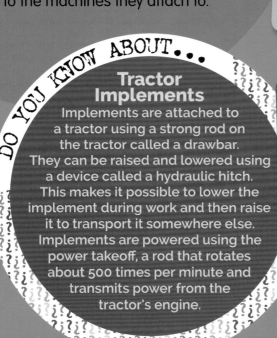

Cultivator

A cultivator is a tractor implement that moves soil. It can be used before crops are planted to loosen the soil or while the crops are growing to kill weeds. Cultivators have to be able to damage weeds without damaging the crops. They consist of metal frames with sharp teeth that dig into the soil. The teeth are pulled backward by the tractor they are attached to.

Planter

Seeder

A seeder can be a tractor implement or a separate machine pushed or pulled by hand. It is used to plant seeds, and there are several different kinds. Broadcast seeders disperse seeds over a large area, but they are not very accurate with the placement of the seeds. Seed drills work for almost all types of seeds, but they can take longer and the dispersal might not be even. Planters are the most accurate and consistent seeder, but they only work for larger seeds.

Combine Harvester

A combine harvester is a machine that collects cereal crops like wheat and barley and separates out the edible part, called the grain, from the rest of the plant, called the chaff. When a combine harvester is driven through a field, it cuts the crops with a device called a cutter bar. Then the crops are sent to the center of the machine where a threshing drum beats them so the grains separate from the chaff. The grains are collected in a tank and the chaff falls out the back of the machine as straw which can be collected later.

Hay Baler

A hay baler is a tractor implement that gathers hay and compresses it into bundles called bales. Bales are easier to transport and store than loose hay. Some hay balers are small and square. They use a plunger to press the hay into the right shape, and then tie it with twine or wire. Other balers are large and round. They use rubber belts to wrap the hay around itself until it is a round bale that can be wrapped. Each type of baler takes under a minute to collect the hay, bale it, and release it.

Machines at Play

Some machines are designed and built solely for entertainment! There is a wide variety of these machines. Some are fixed in a location, and some travel. Some are simple and some are made from many pieces. Some are powered solely by human effort and some are self-propelled with multiple energy sources.

Swing

A swing is powered by human effort. It starts moving when the swinger pumps their legs or is given a push. A swing is a type of simple pendulum, a hanging object that swings back and forth. If it is not interfered with, a pendulum will swing at the same speed continuously. However, swings eventually stop moving if the rider does not keep pumping their legs. This is because air resistance slows them down.

DO YOU KNOW ABOUT...

Inertia and Gravity

Swings would not work without a property called inertia. Inertia means that an object will continue to do the same thing unless an outside force acts on it. If it is moving, it will keep moving. If it is still, it will stay still. Inertia keeps a swing moving and traveling up, and gravity pulls the swing down. Without gravity, you would be able to swing 360 degrees—all the way around!

Coin

Coin moves away

Coin falls into glass

The Great Elephant

Mechanical Elephant

Mechanical elephants are built to mimic living elephants. They walk using gears in their legs and even expel water from their mechanical trunks. There have been two modern mechanical elephants. One was used in a traveling theatre show and the other carries passengers as a ride. Both elephants were built out of steel and wood to weigh over forty tons and stand over thirty feet tall. They are powered using a combination of motors and cylinders. The elephant currently in operation, called The Great Elephant, has a hybrid motor.

Roller Coaster

A roller coaster train does not have an engine or its own power source. After it reaches the top of the first hill of the ride, it is propelled by gravity and momentum. To climb the first hill, most trains use a chain lift, a long looped chain that runs under the track and pulls the train to the top, building up potential energy. For the rest of the roller coaster ride, the train alternates between potential and kinetic energy. It has potential energy when climbing a hill and kinetic energy when falling down the other side. The hills get shorter as the ride continues, because the train gradually loses the energy it had at the beginning due to friction with the track and the air.

Carousel

A carousel is powered by an electric or hydraulic motor. The motor creates rotation in a system of pulleys, belts, gears, shafts, and cranks. This system ultimately turns the entire carousel and moves the animals or objects riders sit on up and down. These objects can be made out of wood, fiberglass, or aluminum.

DO YOU KNOW ABOUT...

Carousel Music
The classic source of carousel music is a small pipe organ called a band organ or fairground organ. It works using bellows, devices that expand to pull in air and contract to blow it out. The bellows send air through the organ's pipes to make music.

Ferris Wheel

A Ferris wheel is a ride that rotates around a central axis. Passengers sit in gondolas or capsules attached to the rim of the wheel. Gondolas and capsules rotate too, which is why the passengers do not go upside down. Ferris wheels are powered by hydraulic motors that rotate tires against the wheel, turning it. Many Ferris wheels are lit at night using bright LED lights.

Machines at Home

So far you have learned about many machines that move outdoors. But some moving machines spend their life cycles inside or near buildings, where they help with everyday tasks like cleaning and telling time.

Ceiling Fan

A ceiling fan has three main parts: a base plate, which connects the fan to the ceiling; the blades of the fan; and a motor. When the fan is turned on, wires carry electricity to the motor, which causes the blades to turn. The blades move the air in the room, but they do not lower its temperature. The reason ceiling fans make people feel cooler is that the movement of the air works like a breeze. It pushes away body heat and evaporates sweat. Some ceiling fans have only two or three blades, and some have as many as ten!

DO YOU KNOW ABOUT...

Paper Fans
Paper fans look very different from ceiling fans, but they work by the same principle. They move air to create a cooling effect without actually cooling the air. But instead of a rotational motion powered by electricity, paper fans have linear movement powered by human effort.

Clock

A clock can be powered by mechanical energy, electric energy, or the kinetic energy of the person using it. Whichever power source a clock uses, the energy causes an object to oscillate, or move back and forth between two points, over and over again. The oscillating objects might be a wheel and pendulum, a quartz crystal, or electrons and atoms. A device called a controller changes the frequency of oscillation into pulses that show time passing. Then a counter chain counts the controller's pulses and converts them into time units, and an indicator displays the time.

Lawn Mower

All lawn mowers have a motor or engine that powers a rotating blade. Rotary lawn mowers need to be pushed by a person. They have either an internal combustion engine or an electric motor and rechargeable battery. This device is connected to an axle that spins a steel blade about 3,000 times per minute. Riding mowers have more powerful engines, because they need to propel themselves in addition to spinning the blade. The blade on a riding mower is connected to the engine with a belt instead of an axle.

Rotary Lawnmover

DO YOU KNOW ABOUT...

Robotic Vacuum Cleaners

Some modern vacuum cleaners are robotic. They have rechargeable batteries and they clean floors without human assistance. Sensors on the robot detect dirt, and a navigation system helps it avoid obstacles.

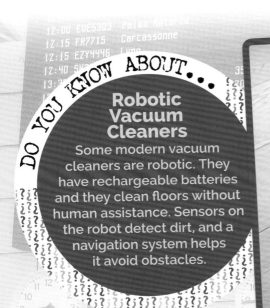

Vacuum Cleaner

A vacuum cleaner is powered by an electric motor. The motor spins a fan to suck air and small dirt particles into the machine and send them into a container like a bag or canister. The air is passed through a filter to remove its particles, which stay behind in the container. Then the cleaner air is released through the back. The clean air is warmer because it picks up heat from the motor as it moves through the vacuum cleaner.

Conveyors

A conveyor is a machine that moves things from one place to another using an endless belt. Some conveyors are simple and flat. Others involve multiple belts, inclines, or modifications for specific jobs.

Conveyor Belt

A conveyor belt is a wide, looped, motor-powered belt. It is attached to two wheels called rotors. When the rotors turn, the friction against the rubber belt causes it to turn too. Cone-shaped rotors are used when the belt needs to curve instead of running straight. Conveyor belts are mostly used for carrying products or materials. They are also used in airports as baggage carousels.

DO YOU KNOW ABOUT....
Moving Sidewalks of the Past and Future

The first moving sidewalk was introduced in 1893 at the World's Fair. The machine started to become more common in the 1950s when airports were expanding. Future moving sidewalks may use the same technology as Maglev rails, allowing them to speed up in the middle of the walkway and slow down at the beginning and end for safety.

Moving Sidewalk

Moving sidewalks are a variation on conveyor belts that transport people instead of objects. They are common in large airports with long distances between terminals. Moving sidewalks sometimes slow down without passengers to save energy and speed up when people approach them. Others stop entirely until they are activated by motion.

Escalator

An escalator is a conveyor with rotating steps instead of a flat belt. It functions as a moving staircase. A motor turns gears that rotate loops of chains, moving the steps. The motor also powers the handrails, which are both narrow rubber conveyor belts. The handrails and steps must move at the same speed for the riders to feel stable. Some escalators always travel in the same direction. Others can be controlled, either by an operator or passenger.

Treadmill

A treadmill is a conveyor for people, like a moving sidewalk or escalator, but it is designed to be used by only one person who is walking or running in place. Treadmills have frames and decks that support the weight of the person on them. The belt portion rotates because of motor-powered rollers. Larger rollers and thicker belts are stronger. Treadmills also include electronic devices, like control panels to adjust speed and incline, and heart rate monitors.

Cable Transport

Cables are strong wires, ropes, or chains used to control a machine. All methods of transportation using cables are called cable transport.

Chairlift

A chairlift transports people up and down a slope. It is made of chairs hanging from a steel cable. Chairlifts are powered by electric motors with diesel engines as backup. They have at least two terminals (one at the top of the slope and one at the bottom). At a terminal, the cable moves around a wheel with the help of pulleys so chairs can travel back in the other direction. There may also be towers between the terminals that help support the cable.

DO YOU KNOW ABOUT...
Types of Chairlifts

There are two types of chairlifts. In fixed grip chairlifts, the chairs are attached to a point on the cable. They have to move at a constant speed. In detachable chairlifts, the chairs are indirectly connected to the cable using devices called grips. Detachable chairlifts can move faster, because the grips can loosen to slow down a chair near a terminal.

Fixed Grip Chairlift

Elevator

Elevator Shaft

An elevator moves people up and down between floors of a building. It is raised and lowered with steel ropes connected to a grooved pulley called a sheave. When the sheave turns, so do the ropes. On the side of the ropes not attached to the elevator is a counterweight. Balancing the weights on both sides of the ropes conserves energy, so the electric motor has less work to do. Some elevators are not cable transport and use hydraulic systems instead.

Zip Line

Zip lines consist of a cable that starts at a high point and ends at a low point. They only transport people in one direction. A pulley system is attached to the cable, and riders use seats or harnesses attached to the pulleys. The rider moves because of the declining slope, and the pulley reduces friction to move them faster. Some zip lines have brake systems, and others slope slightly upward at the end to slow and stop the rider. The longest and fastest zip line is located in South Africa. It is over 6,000 feet long, and it travels at over ninety miles per hour.

DO YOU KNOW ABOUT...

Aerial Tramways

Aerial tramways or aerial trams are a type of cable transport that use ropes to move vehicles called cabins between two points. There are typically two cabins operated at one time. Aerial trams are commonly used at ski destinations or tourist stops.

Funicular

A funicular is like a combination of a train and an elevator. It consists of a car that runs on a very steep track and is pulled by a cable and pulley system. Funiculars run with two cars at the same time so they balance each other, like the counterweight of an elevator. When one funicular car travels down, it helps pull the other car up. Likewise, the car traveling up keeps the car going down from moving too fast. Modern funiculars have motors to assist the process and make up for friction or unbalanced weight in the cars.

Glossary

Artifact – an object made by humans from a previous time period

Astronaut – someone who travels in outer space

Astronomical body – an object in the universe, such as a planet, moon, star, or asteroid

Autonomy – the quality of functioning independently

Bearing – a component that helps machinery move at extremely high speeds

Buoyancy – an upward force on an object in a fluid

Conversion – changing something from one form to another form

Data – statistics and information collected for the purpose of being analyzed

Density – a substance's mass for every unit of volume

Domino effect – one event causing many other similar events to occur one after the other

Earth–moving equipment – a type of construction equipment used to move large amounts of earth

Ecosystem – a community of organisms and their environment

Electromagnetism – magnetic attraction caused by electricity

Element – a chemical substance that cannot be divided into simpler substances

Filter – a device that removes something from a fluid passing through it

Force – the use of energy or strength to influence something

Fossil fuel – a fuel that forms underground from the remains of living things

Friction – a force from two things touching that reduces movement

Generator – a machine that converts mechanical energy into electric energy

Gravity – a downward force that attracts objects to each other

Hatch – an opening found on the deck of a ship that leads to a lower level

Heavier–than–air aircraft – an aircraft that weighs more than the air it is displacing and uses aerodynamic lift or engine lift

Humanoid – having humanlike features

Invent – to create something new

Lighter–than–air aircraft – an aircraft that is filled with a gas that is lighter than the air around it which allows the aircraft to float

Locomotive – a rail vehicle that is self–propelled and used to move railcars

Magma – melted rock from inside the earth

Material–handling equipment – a type of construction equipment used to help with moving, storing, and controlling a variety of products and materials

Mechanical energy – energy related to an object's position and movement

Momentum – a moving object's force, caused by weight and movement

Natural resource – a material that comes from nature and is useful to humans

Non–renewable energy – energy collected from non–renewable energy sources, mainly fossil fuels, that cannot be replenished in the near future or at all

Pendulum – a weight hung from a fixed point so that it can swing back and forth; often used to regulate a clock

Perpendicular – at a ninety–degree angle

Pollute – to make dirty or unsafe

Prototype – the first model of a new design or invention

Public transportation – a system of shared vehicles used by people living in a specific area

Reaction – a change caused by chemicals or the nuclei of atoms interacting with each other

Renewable energy – energy collected from renewable resources, such as wind and sunlight, that can be replenished

Resistance – a force that acts opposite to another force to slow movement

Sensor – a detection device often found on robots and other technology

Sheave – a pulley with a grooved wheel used for hoisting heavy loads

Space walk – an astronaut's activity outside a spacecraft while in space

Technology – a collection of scientific skills and processes used to create goods and services or to accomplish goals

Thrust – a forward force on a vehicle

Torpedo – a type of underwater missile that can be fired from a ship, submarine, or aircraft

Torque – a force that produces rotation

Track – the structure that a train's wheels move on, including one or two rails

Unmanned aerial vehicle – an aircraft operated without a human pilot on board; another name for a drone

Urethane – a synthetic compound used in skateboard wheels and a variety of other products

Vehicle – a machine used for transportation

Index